GOODNIGHT, GOD

A prayer book for children

"GOODNIGHT GOD,
IT'S TIME FOR ME TO PRAY

TO GIVE MY THANKS FOR
WHAT HAS HAPPENED
TODAY!

THANK YOU FOR WAKING ME UP THIS MORNING, FOR MY EYES MY EARS AND NOSE

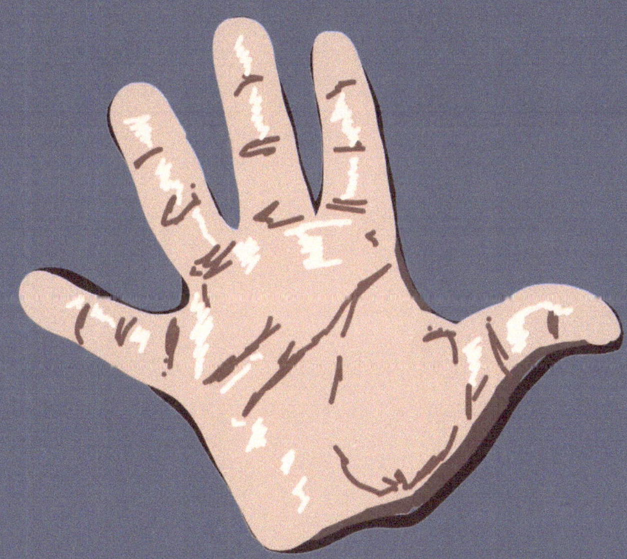
THANK YOU FOR MY
MOUTH, MY FINGERS
AND MY TOES

THANK YOU FOR THE SUN AND HOW IT SHINES IT'S LIGHT

I EVEN THANK YOU FOR THE RAIN, WHEN IT WASN'T THAT BRIGHT

THANK YOU FOR MY
FOOD AND THE WATER
TO WASH IT DOWN

THANK YOU LORD JESUS

FOR ALWAYS BEING

AROUND

THANK YOU FOR ALL
THE FRIENDS THAT YOU
HAVE BROUGHT TO ME

THANK YOU FOR THE FRIENDS THAT I AM YET TO MEET!

THANK YOU FOR THE BUGS AND THE BIRDS IN THE TREES

THANK YOU FOR THE PLANTS AND THE HONEY-MAKING BEES

THANK YOU FOR THIS
SNAIL AS SLIMEY AS
IT IS

FOR I KNOW IT HAS A PURPOSE, BUT I'M NOT SURE WHAT IT IS

THANK YOU FOR THE
LAUGHTER, FOR SMILES
AND MORE

THANK YOU FOR THE
WORLD THAT I'M YET TO
EXPLORE

THANK YOU FOR YOUR GUIDANCE, AND FOR ALL THAT I CAN BE

THANK YOU LORD JESUS FOR PROTECTING ME.

I KNOW IT'S IMPORTANT TO SEEK YOU AND TO PRAY,

TO GIVE THANKS FOR
YESTERDAY,
TOMORROW AND TODAY.

SO GOODNIGHT GOD I'M
THANKFUL FOR YOUR
LOVE,

YOUR BLESSINGS AND
YOUR FAVOUR FROM
THE HEAVENS UP
ABOVE"

AMEN.

DO YOU HAVE ANYTHING
ELSE YOUR THANKFUL FOR?

TAKE SOME TIME TO TELL
GOD AND REMEMBER...

'WHATEVER IS TRUE, HONORABLE, JUST, PURE, LOVELY AND COMMENDABLE. IF THERE IS ANYTHING WORTHY OF PRAISE, THINK ABOUT THESE THINGS'

Philippians | 4:8 | ESV

www.ingramcontent.com/pod-product-compliance
Lightning Source LLC
LaVergne TN
LVHW070239080726
842862LV00019B/340